Creative Writing
in 5 Simple Steps

# Write
# Horror
# Fiction
## in 5 Simple Steps

Laura Baskes Litwin

**Enslow Publishers, Inc.**
40 Industrial Road
Box 398
Berkeley Heights, NJ 07922
USA

http://www.enslow.com

**Library of Congress Cataloging-in-Publication Data**

Litwin, Laura Baskes.
  Write horror fiction in 5 simple steps / Laura Baskes Litwin.
    p. cm. — (Creative writing in 5 simple steps)
  Includes bibliographical references and index.
  Summary: "Divides the creative writing process into five steps, from inspiration to publishable story, and includes in-depth treatment of the horror fiction genre with writing prompts"—Provided by publisher.
  ISBN 978-0-7660-3836-3
  1.  Horror tales—Authorship—Juvenile literature. 2.  Horror tales—Technique--Juvenile literature.  I. Title.
  PN3377.5.H67L57 2012
  808.3'8738—dc22
                                2010038776

Future editions:
Paperback ISBN 978-1-4644-0099-5
ePUB ISBN 978-1-4645-1006-9
PDF ISBN 978-1-4646-1006-6

Printed in the United States of America

032012 Lake Book Manufacturing, Inc., Melrose Park, IL

10 9 8 7 6 5 4 3 2 1

**To Our Readers:** We have done our best to make sure all Internet addresses in this book were active and appropriate when we went to press. However, the author and the publisher have no control over and assume no liability for the material available on those Internet sites or on other Web sites they may link to. Any comments or suggestions can be sent by e-mail to comments@enslow.com or to the address on the back cover.

Every effort has been made to locate all copyright holders of material used in this book.  If any errors or omissions have occurred, corrections will be made in future editions of this book.

♻ Enslow Publishers, Inc., is committed to printing our books on recycled paper. The paper in every book contains 10% to 30% post-consumer waste (PCW). The cover board on the outside of each book contains 100% PCW. Our goal is to do our part to help young people and the environment too!

**Cover and Illustration Credits:** Shutterstock.com

# Contents

# Book Key

### Keeping a Journal

### On the Web

### Genre History

### Fun Fact

### Check It Out!

### Writer's Block

### Here's an Idea!

### Your Assignment

### Organizer

### Daydreaming

# Step 1

## Finding Inspiration

Before Stephen King became the famous and wildly successful author of horror stories that he is today, he worked at various odd jobs in order to scrape together a living wage. One of these jobs was at a commercial laundry in a small town on the coast of Maine, a place where motels, restaurants, and hospitals sent their linens out for washing and folding.

This was not a pleasant job. Crusty dregs of week-old seafood dinner clung to the tablecloths and napkins. Feasting maggots crawled up workers' arms as they loaded the washers. The sheets from the hospitals were covered with maggots, too, but they were sucking on dried blood instead of lobster.

One of Stephen King's coworkers was a man named Harry. By the time King came to work at the laundry, Harry had been there for more than thirty years, despite a horrible accident that happened to him while he was on the job.

In the 1940s, laundry employees were required to wear ties to work. Harry's tie got caught in the gigantic machine that steam pressed and folded the bed sheets. When Harry tried to yank his tangled tie from the equipment, his hand got stuck. When he pulled with his other hand in an effort to rescue himself, that hand got caught as well.

Harry lost both hands, and his arms up to his elbows, in the industrial laundry machine the workers called the mangler. He got steel hooks to replace his missing hands and forearms, and he kept working at the laundromat. As a prank, he liked to run cold water on one hook and hot on the other. Then he would creep up behind busy workers and place his hooks on the backs of their necks.

Harry was the creative inspiration for Stephen King's short story, "The Mangler." In the story, the machine is possessed by a demon, escapes the laundry, and takes madly to the streets. King sold this piece to a magazine and later included it in his first collection of short stories, a book entitled *Night Shift*.

Most of King's other stories and novels do not have such direct inspiration. In fact, King claims he almost never knows where he gets his ideas. "Good story ideas seem to come quite literally from nowhere," he says. "Your job isn't to find these ideas but to recognize them when they show up."[1]

If that sounds daunting, never fear. As King once wisely put it, "The scariest moment is always just before you start. After that, things can only get better."[2]

## What Makes It Horror?

Let's begin by defining what we mean by the genre of horror. A genre is a category, or a style, of art. For our purposes here, the art is literature, and the literature is fiction. In addition to horror, fiction encompasses other genres, including science fiction, fantasy, romance, and mystery.

With horror, a lot of overlap exists with the other genres. It is not always easy to tell the difference between fantasy and horror, or science fiction and horror. Each genre puts its own spin on reality. Each asks the reader to imagine a world altered in some way. For example, a story might feature giant winged rats in outer space. What genre is this? Flying animals are often characters in fantasy, and outer space is usually associated with science fiction. But how about those rats? And did we mention their bloody five-inch fangs?

What horror aims to do differently from other genres is to scare the reader. A familiar situation becomes unfamiliar. An encounter with a strange demon disturbs. In both cases, the reader's pulse quickens. A good horror story is like a good ride at an amusement park. Feeling scared without having to face real danger is exhilarating. The story builds with tantalizing ideas. The reader inches out on the coaster track, knowing the precarious drop is seconds away.

Some horror fiction terrorizes and repulses the reader at the same time. Large flying rats will frighten most people. Adding long fangs that rip human flesh pushes the image past scary to revolting. Now the heart races, and the stomach churns!

One of the most influential writers of horror fiction was a New Englander named H. P. Lovecraft. Lovecraft died, still undiscovered, in 1937. In the years since, however, both his fiction and his studies of the craft of the horror story (what he called "the weird tale") have proven major contributions to the field. Lovecraft wrote, "The oldest and strongest emotion of mankind is fear, and the oldest and strongest kind of fear is fear of the unknown."[3]

# Great Horror Fiction

**WARNING: Many of these books may contain disturbing material and mature themes. Ask your parent or guardian for permission before reading them.**

Mary Shelley—*Frankenstein*
The original mad scientist and his monster

Edgar Allan Poe—"The Tell-Tale Heart"
"What you mistake for madness is but overacuteness of the senses."

Robert Louis Stevenson—*The Strange Case of Dr. Jekyll and Mr. Hyde*
The nightmare of living a double life

Oscar Wilde—*The Picture of Dorian Gray*
Murder and deceit illustrated in a painting

H. G. Wells—*The Island of Dr. Moreau*
The danger of science without compassion

Bram Stoker—*Dracula*
The vampire story against which all others are measured

Henry James—*The Turn of the Screw*
A governess is tormented by ghosts.

H. P. Lovecraft—The Cthulhu Mythos
A shared fictional universe where gods control the fate of mortals

Jack Williamson—*Darker Than You Think*
Small-town reporter versus werewolf

**Shirley Jackson—*The Haunting of Hill House***
A haunted house picks its own tenant.

**Ray Bradbury—*Something Wicked This Way Comes***
A creepy carnival comes to town.

**Richard Matheson—*I Am Legend***
Plague survivors turn into vampires.

**Ira Levin—*Rosemary's Baby***
Is Rosemary having the devil's baby?

**William Peter Blatty—*The Exorcist***
A child possessed by a demon

**Robert McCammon—*Swan Song***
How to save young Swan from the Man of Many Faces

**Stephen King—*Salem's Lot, The Shining, The Stand***
These are three of King's most successful novels.

**Anne Rice—*Interview With the Vampire***
First of the series with very human and sympathetic vampire Lestat

**Dean Koontz—*Phantoms***
The tale of an abandoned ski town

**Christopher Pike—*Remember Me***
Ghosts solving murders

**Neil Gaiman—*The Graveyard Book***
Graveyard ghosts adopt an orphaned baby.

**R. L. Stine—Goosebumps and Nightmare Room series**
Popular series of funny and frightening stories

**Darren Shan—Cirque du Freak series**
Humorous and scary series based on a traveling freak show

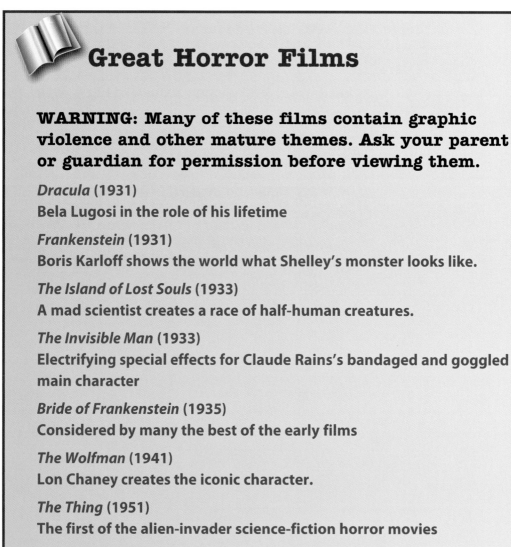

# Great Horror Films

**WARNING: Many of these films contain graphic violence and other mature themes. Ask your parent or guardian for permission before viewing them.**

*Dracula* (1931)
Bela Lugosi in the role of his lifetime

*Frankenstein* (1931)
Boris Karloff shows the world what Shelley's monster looks like.

*The Island of Lost Souls* (1933)
A mad scientist creates a race of half-human creatures.

*The Invisible Man* (1933)
Electrifying special effects for Claude Rains's bandaged and goggled main character

*Bride of Frankenstein* (1935)
Considered by many the best of the early films

*The Wolfman* (1941)
Lon Chaney creates the iconic character.

*The Thing* (1951)
The first of the alien-invader science-fiction horror movies

*Invasion of the Body Snatchers* (1956)
One of the great cult B-movie film-noir classics

*The Blob* (1958)
This film's theme song says it all: "Beware of the blob! It creeps and leaps and slides and glides!"

*Psycho* (1960)
Hitchcock classic; the shower scene may be the most analyzed scene in the history of film.

*The Fall of the House of Usher* (1960)
Famous B-movie filmmaker Roger Corman's first; Vincent Price stars

*The Pit and the Pendulum* (1961)
Corman makes his second movie from a Poe story, and Vincent Price returns.

*The Birds* (1963)
Tippi Hedren and a lot of attacking birds in this Hitchcock classic

*Night of the Living Dead* (1968)
Low-budget black-and-white zombie film by George Romero

*The Exorcist* (1973)
A young girl needs a priest's help after the devil takes over her body.

*The Texas Chainsaw Massacre* (1974)
First of six films featuring serial killer Leatherface

*Jaws* (1975)
Steven Spielberg's famed great white shark story based on Peter Benchley's novel

*Carrie* (1976)
Adapted from Stephen King's novel, the ultimate story of high-school cruelty

*(continued next page)*

*The Omen* (1976)
The first of three movies featuring the satanic child Damien

*Dawn of the Dead* (1978)
Sequel to *Night of the Living Dead*; zombies attempt to take over the world.

*Halloween* (1978)
The first of John Carpenter's hugely popular slasher films

*Alien* (1979)
Stunning special effects create an alien world.

*The Amityville Horror* (1979)
A haunted house based on a true murder story

*Friday the 13th* (1980)
The original in what has become a twelve-movie franchise

*The Shining* (1980)
Stanley Kubrick directs Jack Nicholson in this masterpiece version of King's novel.

*The Thing* (1982)
A remake of the 1951 film, scientists in the Antarctic confront a face-changing alien.

R. L. Stine, the best-selling author of the Goosebumps series, echoes this sentiment: "I was afraid of lots of things— all the basic kinds of fears—afraid of the dark, afraid of going down to the basement. . . . I always thought something would be lurking in the garage. I used to take my bike and just throw it in so I wouldn't have to go in there."[4]

*Poltergeist* (1982)
**First of three movies about the ghost-ridden Freeling family**

*A Nightmare on Elm Street* (1984)
**The first movie of the Freddy Krueger series**

*Child's Play* (1988)
**Chucky is born.**

*Silence of the Lambs* (1991)
**Anthony Hopkins stars as the evil Dr. Hannibal Lecter.**

*The Blair Witch Project* (1999)
**The dark woods provide a scary backdrop for three young filmmakers.**

*Shadow of the Vampire* (2000)
**Fictionalized account of the making of the real 1922 silent horror film**
*Nosferatu*

*Trick 'r Treat* (2008)
**Four interwoven stories about the dark secrets of a small town**

*Paranormal Activity* (2009)
**A suburban couple deals with a nightly demon.**

Stine explains that the fears he endured as a child have had an enormous impact on his writing. "That's a painful way to go through childhood, I think, having all these fears . . . but in a way, it's kind of lucky. It helped me out later, because now, when I write these scary books for kids, I can think back to that feeling of panic. I can remember what it felt like."[5]

Perhaps without even realizing it, many parents initiate their children in the horror club at a young age. The famous fairy tales collected by Jacob and Wilhelm Grimm are just that—grim. They include gruesome stories of children being eaten by wolves, such as in "Little Red Riding Hood," or pursued by evil witches, as in "Hansel and Gretel." In "Cinderella," the evil stepsisters cut off parts of their feet to fit into the glass slipper. The dancer in Hans Christian Anderson's "The Red Shoes" gets her feet chopped off just because she takes a break.

Stine recalls, "My introduction to scary literature was *Pinocchio*. My mother read it to me every day when I was three or four. The original Pinocchio is terrifying. First he smashes Jiminy Cricket to death with a wooden mallet. Then he goes to sleep with his feet up on the stove and burns his feet off! I never forgot it!"[6]

But is scaring kids—or anyone else—a bad thing? Judging from the sales of Goosebumps books alone (more than 100 million copies sold, more than a million per month[7]), it appears not a lot of people think so.

Without a doubt, many people enjoy being frightened by books and movies. The story may be unsettling, but the crucial fact remains: it is only a story. Like the joyous relief of waking from an awful nightmare to your sun-dappled bedroom, a terrifying horror story is only a fiction.

What works best in horror storytelling? Even at its most shocking or grisly, a good horror story should entertain the reader and provide him or her with an escape from the everyday. If the author wants to use ghosts or carnival freaks or serial killers to do this, all's fair.

# How to Horrify

Horror stories should be disturbing. Loss of control or power is an important recurring theme, as is death, or isolation and alienation. At the core of many a horror story, something is unknowable. A well-written story will set up an uncertain difficult situation and allow the protagonist, or central character, to overcome it.

The main character needs to triumph over the bad stuff in order for the story to ultimately succeed. The writer need not gloss over the dark side. In fact, most of your story can hover over there, but make sure your hero or heroine gains some control in the end. Remember, the reader wants to wake up from the nightmare.

This does not mean that your story must have a happy ending. What is required is that your main character do something—and it can be a shocking, terrible thing, this is horror we're talking about—that ties the story together in a way the reader can believe.

Now, about coming up with ideas for characters and stories: start with the basics. Because you want to write a scary story, ask yourself the question: what are you afraid of? Presumably you fear more than just one or two things. Go ahead and make a list.

If you scribble your list on a napkin, or a scrap sheet of paper, stash it in a drawer for safekeeping. Story ideas are valuable. Even when you are absolutely certain you will not forget that best-ever idea, you just might. In fact, you probably will, and it's a frustrating feeling.

Even better than a solo piece of paper for your story ideas is a pad or notebook. It doesn't need to be very big. Keep it with you so you can jot down ideas—even half-baked ones—when they occur to you. Leave it next to your bed in case you wake up from a dream (or better yet, a nightmare) with some scary good ideas!

## Get Started!

See what kind of scary stories you can come up with using each of these writing prompts. Start with just a few simple sentences and see if you are able to tease out a bigger, better idea. Some ideas will flow more easily than others. One of them might prove worthy of becoming a longer story.

1.  The school bus arrives to pick you up, but your regular driver is not at the wheel. A strange-looking substitute opens the door and beckons you to climb in.

2.  The three-mile loop you run every morning suddenly looks completely unfamiliar. But how could you have made a wrong turn?

3.  Third down, you enter the huddle. Wait, who are these grim-faced guys under the helmets . . . what happened to your teammates?

4.  The elevator opens, and you get in without paying attention. The door closes, and you suddenly notice the three unsmiling men dressed identically in dark suits and mirrored sunglasses.

5. You receive a text from an unknown number warning you that "something is coming."

6. The fortune-teller turns over the tarot card and gasps. "I'm sorry," she says. "We're done here."

7. Ice fishing with your brother, you see something frozen below you. It is not a fish.

8. You get home from school to find the back door slightly ajar. You enter an empty kitchen . . . why isn't the dog waiting with his usual friendly wag?

9. You receive a picture message on your phone. You recognize yourself in the photo . . . but who is that strange man with you?

10. As part of a sorority or fraternity initiation, you allow yourself to be left blindfolded in a closet. Something furry brushes up against your ankle.

# Step 2

## Planning and Research

Keeping a notebook with a list of story ideas in progress is a useful tool. One of the greatest advantages of the list is that you will have good ideas at the ready. When you finally sit down to write, it will be that much easier to get your story under way with the seed of a good idea in hand.

Your list of fears is not going to be exactly like the next person's. Different things strike terror in different people. But certain fears are more common than others. A lot of people are afraid of the dark, for example, or of snakes, or of being trapped. How can you be certain that your horror story will be different from someone else's if you write about the same scary things?

Take a deep breath. No worries. Your imagination is a unique and wonderful thing. Your story about being stuck in an elevator is absolutely going to be different from the next person's if you let loose your imagination.

The idea is just the starting point. Pay careful attention to the details and make the idea your own. Cause the numbers to suddenly disappear on your elevator's buttons. Change the piped Muzak (elevator music) to a sinister minor chord. Describe the wall panels warping and moving in on your hero. Turn the fellow who joined him on the seventh floor into a zombie.

# Some Truths

The first truth is that there are as many good horror stories yet to be written as there are good writers with nimble imaginations. The second truth is that some very good horror stories have already been written. If you want to write good horror fiction, first you need to read it.

You need to read a whole lot of it. The more horror fiction you read, the better your own will become. Go to the library or the bookstore and find books by Shirley Jackson, Richard Matheson, or Robert McCammon. These are just three great authors; there are dozens more. Works by some of the best writers, such as Ray Bradbury, might be filed under different genres, such as science fiction. But Bradbury's *Something Wicked This Way Comes* is as excellent a creepy tale as any you will ever read.

By reading the best authors, you get free lessons at the feet of the masters. Reading good literature helps immensely in writing good literature. Without even realizing it, you will model some of your writing in the fashion of the greats.

What's more, you will get a sense of what ideas work, as well as what has already been done. It is important that you know what stories are out there already. You want yours to be original. You can still write a monster story, but it has to be different from the other monster stories.

Read the horror classics, such as *Frankenstein* and *Dracula*. In 1816, Mary Wollstonecraft Shelley was only nineteen years old when she wrote *Frankenstein*. She explained that the idea for the book came to her in a dream:

*When I placed my head on my pillow, I did not sleep, nor could I be said to think. . . . I saw the hideous phantasm of a man stretched out, and then, on the working of some powerful engine, show signs of life and stir with an uneasy, half-vital motion.*[1]

Before Shelley, there was no mad scientist creating a monster in his laboratory. In the almost two centuries since its publication, *Frankenstein* has given rise to many imitators. But there has only ever been one true Frankenstein monster.

Many vampire tales existed before *Dracula*. Vampires appeared in the earliest recorded folklore of almost every world culture. But Bram Stoker's novel, published in 1897, is the vampire tale against which all modern versions are compared. What makes him scarier than earlier vampires is his unpredictable evil nature. He has a huge appetite and attacks at random. Although physical violence occurs often in the book, it is *Dracula*'s psychological terror that sets it apart.

Do not be shy about trying to write your own monster tale. Use a vampire, ghost, or werewolf, but just be sure to make it your own with unique characteristics. You can rejuvenate the old monsters, but you do not want to duplicate them.

What you should try to keep true to, however, are some of the more well-known "facts" about your monster. Even if you decide to twist some of these facts to make your demon distinctive, you should not ignore Basic Vampire 101: he drinks blood, he shuns daylight, and he sleeps in a coffin. Your vampire may sleep in a Cadillac, but to make him believable, you need to be able to explain why your guy is different from his relatives.

# Decisions, Decisions

So how are you finally going to decide what to write about? Maybe you have heard a teacher say before, "Write what you know." This is often good advice. It does not mean you have to write about what you like. In truth, sometimes the best writing ends up being about what you hate. It is easier to describe how much you despise boiled brussels sprouts than it is to describe how much you love chocolate chip cookie dough ice cream. Try it, you'll see.

If you write about what you know, you will do a better job of getting the nitty-gritty details right. Someone who grows up on a dairy farm is going to be better able to describe milking a cow—and the smell of the barn and the weight of the full pail—than someone who grows up in a brownstone in the Bronx.

If you know a lot about electric trains, you can make your killer a collector of them and locate your story in his dark basement. The narrative will move along nicely, with meaty details about the guy's 0-8-0 steam locomotive Pennsylvania Flyer with an operating headlight.

But when the action leaves the train tracks, you might find you want to do a little background research—not a lot necessarily, but enough to make your story believable and more interesting. When the electric train collector-killer ties up his victim, you might want to describe the gauge of the rope or the type of knot he uses. Neither of these things is too difficult to learn about with a little research.

In general terms, perhaps the best advice might be to start with what you know and then research what you do not. The library is a good place to begin when you need to do some digging on a subject. The librarian is your expert. Ask him or her for help with books, periodicals, or Internet research.

You should search online yourself for research material also. The Internet is an amazingly helpful research instrument. What you need to be wary of at all times, however, is what Web site you use for information. Not all sites are as reliable as others. A Web site with a domain name ending in .edu or .gov is managed by an educational or governmental institution, making it more likely—though by no means certain—to have accurate information.

# Step 3

## Organization

Whether you are jotting down thoughts or researching topics for your story, you want to create a system for yourself that helps you stay organized. There is no single perfect system. What works for one writer may or may not work for the next. But organizing your notes in some fashion is really important.

## Getting It Together

You may already have decided to safeguard your good ideas in a notebook. Perhaps some of these good ideas seem like bad ideas, but do not cross them out with a heavy black marker! They may be just what you want the next go-around.

Using bright-colored pens or highlighters can be key in helping organize your notebook. Assign each character its own color, or you may prefer to color code by main ideas.

Index cards are a tried-and-true method for organization as well. Keep it simple: just one idea per card. Cut the cards in half to save paper. You do not need to write in full sentences. You may end up with a bunch of cards, but it will streamline your effort when you start writing.

If you take notes from books or the Internet, the index cards are a good place to record where you found your information. Write down the page number or the Internet address carefully.

Let's say you decide to give your murderer a twelve-inch Bowie hunting knife. You know the blade is steel, but you are not exactly sure how to describe the handle. You can find a book on the subject, such as *The Bowie Knife: Unsheathing an American Legend* (Andrew Mowbray, Inc., 2004), or you could do a Web search on hunting blades.

Both are legitimate references, and whichever one you decide to use is fine. Just be certain to cite it in your story. If you use someone else's words or information, you need to give the person credit for it.

You never want to plagiarize, even by accident. Accidental plagiarism can happen when you do not even realize you are using someone else's words or ideas. When you take notes from a source, either copy the words exactly and use quotation marks, or very carefully select different words to express a similar idea.

 ## Outlining

Once you think you have most of your ideas formulated in your head, and most of the research behind you, it is a good idea to sketch out at least a rough form of your story in an outline.

The outline is just a framework. You can deviate from it when you dive into the writing, but it helps a lot while you are in that feverish creative state or suffering from writer's block if you have an outline to which to refer.

With horror fiction, it is especially important to figure out your ending before you start. When you know where your story is going, you will do a much better job of bringing your reader along with you for the scary ride.

R. L. Stine explains, "I think of the ending first. . . . I know the ending, so then I can always get there. . . . [B]efore I start to write, I know everything that's going to happen in the book. I have it all planned, and then I can just enjoy the writing. I've done all the hard part. I've done the thinking before I start to write."[1]

Making an outline requires more effort before you start but allows you to do less once you get into the thick of it. A first-rate terror tale is a skin-crawling mystery that grabs your reader and doesn't let him or her go. You need to organize your story, working backward from the end, to make certain all the elements leading to the conclusion make sense.

Exactly what are these elements? In the most basic terms, you can break down the elements of a horror story to its setting, characters, and plot. Each element connects with the other: under a full moon (setting), the werewolf (character) attacks the drive-in movie crowd (plot).

## Setting

Perhaps more than any other genre, horror relies on setting. Creating an atmosphere of tension and suspense is crucial to a successful horror story. To do a good job with this, think about how each of your senses can contribute.

# CHARACTER SKETCHES

Like many of Stephen King's novels, *Salem's Lot* makes use of a large cast of characters, and even the minor figures pack a punch. The old man who runs the town dump has the vivid name of Dud Rogers: "He was a hunchback with a curious cocked head that made him look like God had given him a final petulant wrench before allowing him out into the world. . . . Dud liked the dump. . . . The dump was Disneyland and Shangri-La rolled up into one. . . . The best part was the fires—and the rats."[2]

Make lists of traits for each of your characters before you start writing. Your hero should not be a perfect guy because he will be boring then, too. On the flip side, it can be interesting to give your monster some endearing qualities. Think different, odd, new. Here are some ideas to get you started:

**GIVE HIM/HER A NAME**
   formal ones and toss in a nickname

**FIGURE WHAT HE/SHE LOOKS LIKE**
   picture someone you know, someone you pass on the street, look in a magazine

For example, picture yourself in a Greyhound bus terminal at two in the morning on a sweltering August night, in-the-middle-of-nowhere Nebraska. A single fan drones overhead, barely moving the heavy air. Cigarette butts litter a cracked linoleum floor. Outside the window, the silent pitch-black plains stretch in four directions, with no sign of the scheduled bus, or any other traffic. A morbidly obese woman presses her

**WHERE HE/SHE LIVES**
cave, hot-air balloon, apartment, trailer park, army base

**FRIENDS AND FAMILY**
parents, siblings, best friend, significant other, pets

**WHAT HE/SHE DOES FOR A LIVING**
professor, chimney sweep, nurse, dog trainer, jockey

**WHAT HE/SHE DOES FOR FUN**
archery, bake, surf, read, photography

**WHAT HE/SHE NEVER WANTS TO DO**
grocery shop, get on an airplane, celebrate his birthday, cry, tuck in his shirt

**TALENTS**
pie-eating, oboe, chess, kickboxing, poetry

**FLAWS**
nervous, forgetful, cranky, stubborn, lazy

sweaty flesh against yours on the waiting-room bench. You take a bite from a tuna fish sandwich that went bad from the heat hours earlier.

Your story can continue in many directions from here, but an atmosphere of bleak menace is a nice attention grabber. Your reader's curiosity and anxiety levels will start inching up from the start.

Now let's turn our attention to the enormously overweight woman. She is wearing a loose-fitting, brown sleeveless smock. The exposed skin on her beefy arms and legs is badly bruised. A plastic bracelet on her wrist identifies her as a patient from the local psychiatric institution.

Your heart pumps faster. Why is she at the bus depot alone, in the middle of the night, still in her hospital gown? And why, in a nearly empty lobby, is she sitting so close that you can smell her bad breath?

After you set the stage, let your characters tell your story. Aim to create three-dimensional characters, so real they seem to think for themselves. Consider what they look like but also what they grab for snacks, what music they listen to, where their grandparents were born. Can they swim? Are they afraid of heights? Allergic to bees?

## Your Characters

Before you start writing, make detailed lists of each of your characters' major and minor traits. Pretend you are interviewing them. Get to know them well enough that you know their opinions on things and how they will react in different circumstances. Listen to how they speak. A teenage skateboarder will not sound like a retired army colonel.

If you create full-blown living-and-breathing characters, they will help you write your plot. Believe it or not, plotting, the last element of story crafting, is in some ways the easiest.

To plot your story, pose a question and let your characters answer it. What if the overweight woman escaped from the lunatic asylum? Maybe she is sitting inappropriately near because she is about to grab you around the neck in a stranglehold. Or maybe she's not nuts at all. Maybe her evil brother committed her against her will in order to inherit the family business. Her jujitsu training will come in handy when she commandeers the next bus. The possibilities for plot are limitless. Sketch your characters with care, and more often than not, they will tell you what happens next.

## Finding a Hook

You want to hook and reel in your reader with the first few paragraphs of your story. Figuring out how to get your reader interested enough to stick with you is part technique and part enthusiasm. The second part is easy: if you are excited about what you write, the reader will sense it. It will be evident in the vivid descriptions and intriguing tone of your writing.

Perfecting the technique takes a bit more work. Let's practice technique here. Using these prompts, try writing opening paragraphs of three to four sentences each:

1. At the tailgate before the football game, Joe begins choking on the foot-long hot dog he crammed hungrily down his throat. He knows he should signal for help, but that seems so uncool. As he starts to lose consciousness, Joe reconsiders his options . . . dorky or dead?

2. MISSING CHEF'S BODY FOUND IN FREEZER
The body of French chef Jean-Louis du Champignon was discovered Monday evening hanging in the walk-in freezer of his famed New York City bistro, The Mushroom Man. Du Champignon had been reported missing by his longtime girlfriend early last week. An anonymous source reports that the corpse showed signs of mutilation, but police refused to comment.

3. The cemetery gate was missing a hinge, and the iron door swung open easily. The damp mossy ground felt soft underfoot, and the path to the crypt looked recently tended. As the flashlight dimmed, Cassandra cursed herself for not changing the batteries before leaving home. If they just didn't have to go below ground. Entering that cold marble chamber was what she dreaded most. Just how secret did this meeting have to be anyway?

4. "Are you kidding me?" Tina asked. "No one's been in there for ten years at least." "That's why we're going to be the first," responded Drew. "We'll find the old man's remains, and the family will fork over the reward money." "What makes you think anyone is even left to pay us after all this time?" "I don't know for sure." Drew shrugged. "But I can already see my pretty mug in the newspaper." "Are you alive or dead in that picture?" Tina muttered.

# Step 4

## Write, Write, Write

You dreamed up some bloodcurdling plot for your story. Then you did some research where necessary, organized your notes, worked hard at sketching out your characters, and mapped out a general outline. You are ready to start writing this thing!

Whether you now grab some clean sheets of paper and a pen or boot up the computer is your call. It is more important to find a quiet, comfortable place to work. Unless you are home alone, the kitchen table is not a choice location. Neither is the TV room. You need a spot without distractions.

A common piece of advice offered to new writers is to "write every day at the same time." This is a good suggestion for the most part. Find time to write every day. Even the shortest bit of writing will hone your skills. Go to your desk when you can, but keep a small notepad in your backpack for those chance moments of inspiration or for those umpteen times in any day when you are stuck waiting for something or someone.

Do not fret about it being the exact same time every day. Particularly when you are in school, it is hard to stick to a prescribed schedule. Homework and other activities will have to take priority at times. More important than the scheduled time of day for writing is the regular activity of doing it.

In his book, *On Writing*, Stephen King urges, "If you want to be a writer, you must do two things above all others: read a lot and write a lot. There's no way around these two things that I'm aware of, no shortcut."[1]

King describes the value of what he calls "writing with the door closed and open."[2] Slam the door shut for the first effort, he counsels. By this, he means write the first draft of your story without any outside help. Let the words and ideas be yours and yours alone. When you decide you are satisfied with the writing—and only then—open the door and let someone else read it as well.

## Show Versus Tell

Remember the game "Show and Tell?" Your writing will be that much stronger if you learn how to show instead of merely tell. Telling gives your reader information without much life or zip to it. Showing goes beyond the surface and allows your reader to visualize exactly what it is you want him or her to see.

For an example, this is telling: in Japan, census workers miscounted an elderly man who had died earlier. This is showing: A man, previously believed to be one of Japan's oldest at 111 years, was found in his bed last evening by unsuspecting census workers, an apparent mummy for more than three decades. The well-preserved corpse was clothed in simple gray pajamas and weighed approximately ten pounds.

# STEPHEN KING'S "TOOLBOX"

In his book, *On Writing*, Stephen King suggests writers mentally visualize a carpenter's three-shelved toolbox as a storage case for their writing tools.

Vocabulary goes on the top level of the toolbox. Stick with plain honest words, King says: "One of the really bad things you can do to your writing is to dress up the vocabulary, looking for longer words because you're maybe a little ashamed of your short ones. This is like dressing up a household pet in evening clothes."[3]

On the same shelf next to the vocabulary, put some grammar. Again, King argues, don't make it complicated: "One who does grasp the rudiments of grammar finds a comforting simplicity at its heart, where there need be only nouns, the words that name, and verbs, the words that act."[4]

King dedicates the entire second shelf of the toolbox to *The Elements of Style* by William Strunk Jr. and E. B. White. He says, "I'll tell you right now that every aspiring writer should read *The Elements of Style* because it teaches the basics of writing simply and clearly."[5]

The last shelf is reserved for the work of the writer: "Build a paragraph at a time, constructing these of your vocabulary and your knowledge of grammar and basic style. . . . [Do] we not agree that sometimes the most basic skills create things far beyond our expectations?"[6]

# Point of View

Another important technique a writer must take into account is point of view. The point of view is "the eyes" behind how your story is presented to the reader. In a first-person point of view, your character will refer to himself as "I," as in "I bought a ticket to the slasher film." The second-person point of view uses "you," as in "you bought a ticket to the slasher film." The most commonly used point of view, and in many ways the most flexible, is third person, as in "Celia bought a ticket to the slasher film."

One additional point of view to consider—one you might want to give to a supernatural demon—is the omniscient narrator. Omniscient means "all-knowing." This narrator knows what is going on in every character's head. This makes him powerful, but it makes it difficult to build suspense in your story when every thought is made known to the reader. Because building suspense is fundamental to the success of your horror story, you might not want to let all the cats out of the bag with an omniscient voice.

# Suspense

Two principal techniques help build suspense. A basic tool of horror fiction is "suspending disbelief" in your reader. This means creating a situation or understanding in which your reader is able to believe that an unlikely situation can really happen.

In Robert Louis Stevenson's famous story *The Strange Case of Dr. Jekyll and Mr. Hyde*, the main character drinks a potion to transform himself from the virtuous Dr. Jekyll to the villainous Mr. Hyde. The reader may not really believe in the powers of a magic potion but can readily suspend disbelief by reminding himself that people do in fact have good and bad sides or lead double lives.

Suspense also can be escalated by using cliff-hangers. A cliff-hanger is a plot device that leaves characters in precarious danger just at the point when the narrative takes a break. If your story has chapters, ending one with a cliff-hanger can be effective. The reader will want to keep reading to find out where the story is heading next.

Okay, you are set. Time now to do what King suggests. Close the door and start writing. Because this first attempt is a rough draft, you do not need to worry about making it perfect. You will have plenty of opportunity for rewriting at a later date, once your story is complete. For the moment, let your imagination fly!

## Writing Dialogue

You want the dialogue in your story to sound realistic in order to suck your reader into your frightening world. You know not everyone sounds alike. People of different ages or cultures naturally speak differently. They have different accents, vocabularies, and tones of voice. By paying careful attention to word choice and speech pattern, you can write dialogue that can help create three-dimensional characters.

Try these prompts:

1. Record a conversation between two people. Then, without transcribing it word-for-word, write it down. Try to bring your reader in as if he, too, were present at the time. Make sure it is clear at all times who is speaking. Even the tiniest details are important: Did both people speak at the same speed? Did one use slang? Did one interrupt the other? Did an airplane overhead muffle some words?

2. You are the world-famous magician The Great Tortellini. While you appear to cut your beautiful assistant in half, you distract your audience with rapid-fire patter. Write a paragraph using this entertaining smooth talk.

3. Your mom catches you stuffing your face with the cookies she has just baked for her book group. Let's hear the conversation.

# Step 5

## Publishing Your Work

Getting a first draft down on paper is exciting. When your ideas start flowing, sometimes it is hard to write or type fast enough. With a rough draft, your aim is to get the basic story right. With the final step, revising your work, your goal is to polish it until it gleams.

Have you ever heard the phrase "the devil is in the details"? This sounds particularly appropriate for a horror story doesn't it? What it means is that you want to do a careful and thorough job with your story. You can focus on the big picture with your rough draft, but pay close attention to the tiniest of details when you revise.

Revising your story can mean refining words or phrases, combining or deleting ideas, or even fixing facts. It involves editing your story to make certain your sentences are written clearly. It most definitely includes proofreading to check for mistakes in spelling and grammar.

When you finally think you have made your story as good as it can get (and you can promise yourself you are not settling for nearly-as-good-as-it-can-get because you cannot bear another stab at revising), then it is time to make it ready for publishing.

# MANUSCRIPT FORMATTING GUIDELINES

Before you submit your story, make certain it conforms to the basic rules of manuscript formatting. They are as follows:

The hard copy of your story should be double-spaced on white, hefty 8.5" by 11" paper. Use black ink in a plain twelve-point font such as Times New Roman. Print on only one side of the page and leave a one-inch margin on all sides.

You do not need a separate title page, and the first page should include your contact information—home and e-mail addresses, plus telephone number—in the upper left-hand corner. In the right-hand corner, put the number of words in your story. On all the pages but the first one, have a header with your name, the story's title, and a page number to safeguard against your story's getting lost or disordered.

Both print and Web publishers have guidelines, or rules, for content and formatting. First, find out what kind of stories the publication wants. Then, read and follow carefully the manuscript formatting guidelines for any publication you consider. Improperly formatted stories may not get read at all.

Although submission guidelines may seem like hard work, think of all the hard work that preceded them. Stephen King quotes a writer friend of his as saying, "You can't make them like your story, but you can at least make it easy for them to try to like it."[1]

Because many publishing houses, in particular the larger ones, will not accept unsolicited stories, you might want to ask a literary agent to represent you. You will need to follow specific submission guidelines with an agent as well. You can contact more than one agent at a time to see if they are interested, but do not submit writing to more than one at a time.

Numerous Web sites welcome student fiction, and many of them are dedicated to the horror genre. Self-publishing Web sites are an excellent alternative to traditional publishers. You can publish your story online using one of many such services on the Internet. The costs and services offered vary, so be sure to check what they provide.

Be persistent. Be tough. You will get work rejected. Everyone does. It is extremely rare for an author to get a book deal on the first try. But be fearless. You write horror—it goes with the territory!

# Chapter Notes

### Step 1: Finding Inspiration

1. Stephen King, *On Writing: A Memoir of the Craft* (New York: Simon & Schuster, 2000), p. 25.
2. Ibid., p. 274.
3. H. P. Lovecraft, "The Appeal of the Unknown," *Supernatural Horror in Literature* (New York: B. Abramson, 1945), p. 128.
4. "Transcript From an Interview With R. L. Stine," *Reading Rockets*, 2008, <http://www.readingrockets.org/books/interviews/stine/transcript> (September 18, 2011).
5. Ibid.
6. "Author Interview: R. L. Stine," *Harper Collins Publishers*, 2010, <http://www.harpercollins.com/author/authorExtra.aspx?authorID=14471&displayType=interview> (September 18, 2011).
7. "Goosebumps Series Summary," *eNotes*, 2011, <http://www.enotes.com/goosebumps-series-salem/goosebumps-series> (September 18, 2011).

### Step 2: Planning and Research

1. Mary Shelley, *Frankenstein* (New York: Penguin Classic Edition, 1992), p. 9.

### Step 3: Organization

1. "Interview With R. L. Stine," *The Author Hour*, 2010, <http://theauthorhour.com/r-l-stine/> (September 18, 2011).
2. Stephen King, *Salem's Lot* (New York: Simon & Schuster, 1975), pp. 62–63.

## Step 4: Write, Write, Write

1. Stephen King, *On Writing: A Memoir of the Craft* (New York: Simon & Schuster, 2000) p. 139.
2. Ibid., p. 210.
3. Ibid., p. 110.
4. Ibid., p. 114.
5. Ibid., pp. xviii, 122.
6. Ibid., pp. 130–131.

## Step 5: Publishing Your Work

1. Stephen King, *On Writing: A Memoir of the Craft* (New York: Simon & Schuster, 2000), p. 248.

# Glossary

**cite**—To give proper credit to an authority or reference.

**deviate**—To stray from a previous course.

**format**—The organization or plan of the manuscript.

**gauge**—Dimension or size.

**genre**—A category or style of art.

**hone**—To sharpen or improve to make more effective.

**legitimate**—Reasonable and logical; in accordance with established standards.

**menace**—Something that threatens to cause evil, harm, or injury.

**narrative**—The story or account of events and the technique of telling it.

**nitty-gritty**—Essential and basic.

**phantasm**—A creation of the imagination, an apparition, or fantasy.

**plagiarize**—To use someone else's ideas or words without giving him or her credit.

**point of view**—The perspective from which a story is presented. There is the first-person point of view ("I am leaving"), second-person point of view ("You are leaving"), and third-person point of view ("She is leaving).

**protagonist**—The leading character or hero in a story.

**psychological**—Relating to the will or the mind rather than the body.

**rejuvenate**—To make new or fresh.

**rudiments**—Basics.

**theme**—The dominant or unifying idea of a story.

**umpteen**—Indefinite, countless.

**unsolicited**—Supplied without being requested.

**visualize**—To recall or form mental images or pictures.

# Further Reading

### Books

Farrell, Tish. *Be a Creative Writer*. Tunbridge Wells, Kent, England: TickTock Books, Ltd., 2010.

Hamilton, John. *Horror (You Write It!)*. Edina, Minn.: ABDO and Daughters, 2009.

Knost, Michael, ed. *Writers Workshop of Horror*. Chapmanville, W.Va.: Woodland Press, 2009.

### Internet Addresses

**The World of R. L. Stine**
http://rlstine.com/#nav/home

**The Nightmare Room**
http://thenightmareroom.com/

**StephenKing.com**
http://www.stephenking.com/index.html

**Horror Writers Association**
http://www.horror.org/

**The Literary Gothic**
http://www.litgothic.com/index_fl.html

# Addendum

## Great Sources for Horror Lovers

### Monster Librarian
http://www.monsterlibrarian.com/

### Library Thing
http://www.librarything.com/subject/Horror+stories

## Finding a Literary Agent

Here are some Web sites that may be helpful in locating a literary agent.

### Agent Query
http://www.agentquery.com/

### Association of Authors' Representatives
http://aaronline.org/

### Firstwriter.com
http://www.firstwriter.com/

### The Agent List
http://www.katfeete.net/writing/agents.html

# Where to Publish Your Horror Story

**NOTE: Be sure to check what services and costs are associated with each source.**

## GENERAL INFORMATION & MARKET GUIDES

**Hellnotes**
http://hellnotes.com/

**Horror Factor**
http://horror.fictionfactor.com/

**Horror Writers Association**
http://www.horror.org

**Novel & Short Story Writer's Market**
http://www.novelandshortstory.com/

## SMALL PRINT PUBLISHERS SPECIALIZING IN HORROR

**Cemetery Dance Publications**
http://www.cemeterydance.com/

**Delirium Books**
http://www.deliriumbooks.com/

**Earthling Publications**
http://www.earthlingpub.com/

**Night Shade Books**
http://www.nightshadebooks.com/

## PRINT AND ONLINE SOURCES

**Amazing Kids**
http://www.amazing-kids.org/fiction

**The Blue Pencil Online**
http://www.thebluepencil.net/

**Cicada Magazine**
http://www.cicadamag.com/

**Launch Pad Magazine**
http://www.launchpadmag.com/

**Teen Ink**
http://www.teenink.com/

## SELF-PUBLISHING WEB SITES

**Blurb**
http://www.blurb.com/

**Calaméo**
http://www.calameo.com/

**iUniverse**
http://www.iuniverse.com/

**Lulu**
http://www.lulu.com/

**Scribd**
http://www.scribd.com/

# Index

## A
atmosphere, 25, 27

## C
characters
    dialogue, 35–36
    overview, 28–29
    sketches of, 26–27
cliff-hangers, 35

## D
*Dracula* (Stoker), 20

## F
fairy tales, 14
fantasy, 7
*Frankenstein* (Shelley),
    19–20

## G
genre, 6, 7, 19, 25, 39
Goosebumps (Stine), 12, 14
grammar, 33

## H
horror
    book list, 8–9
    film list, 10–13
    overview, 6–7, 12–14
    themes in, 15

## I
index cards, 23–24
inspiration, 5–6

## K
King, Stephen, 5–6, 26, 32,
    33

## L
Lovecraft, H. P., 7

## M
"The Mangler" (King), 6

## N
*Night Shift* (King), 6
notebooks, 16, 18, 23

## O
organization
    hook, 29–30
    outlining, 24–25
    overview, 23–24
    setting, 25–28

## P
plagiarism, 24
planning, research
    ideas, tracking, 15–16,
        18
    reading in, 19–20
    subject knowledge in,
        21–22
publishing
    literary agents, 39
    overview, 37–39
    self-publishing, 39
    submission guidelines,
        38, 39

## R
references, recording, 24
resources
    books, 8–9
    films, 10–13
    Web sites, 22
    writing tools, 33

## S
*Salem's Lot* (King), 26
science fiction, 7
Shelley, Mary, 19–20
*Something Wicked This Way*
    *Comes* (Bradbury), 19
Stine, R. L., 12–14, 25

## V
vocabulary, 33

## W
writing
    basic tools of, 33
    dialogue, 35–36
    overview, 31–32
    plotting, 28–29
    point of view, 34
    revisions, 37
    show vs. tell, 32
    suspense, 34–35
writing prompts, 16–17,
    29–30, 36